HF454161

ISBN: 978-2-9047-2349-0

Published in Nigeria in 2023 by Prodigy Press

81 Adeshina street,
Ijeshatedo,
Surulere, Lagos

Cover Design by BrightMedia

A catalogue record of this book will be available from the National Library of Nigeria.

NAVIGATING THE BUSINESS MAZE

Essential Management Skills for Today's Leade

Timothy O. Enitinwa

Table of Contents

Managing Your Expectations

In an era marked by rapid technological advancements and shifting economic landscapes, the role of a manager transcends the traditional boundaries of supervising teams and managing resources. Today's leaders are expected to navigate complex challenges, drive innovation, and inspire their teams to achieve unprecedented success. "Navigating the Business Maze: Essential Management Skills for Today's Leaders" is a pivotal guide that equips current and aspiring managers with the tools and insights necessary to thrive in the dynamic world of modern management.

This book was born out of a recognition that the skills required to lead effectively are both diverse and complex. It addresses the multifaceted aspects of management, from strategic decision-making and ethical leadership to financial acumen and conflict resolution. Each chapter is crafted not only to provide theoretical knowledge but also to offer practical strategies and real-world applications that leaders can immediately implement. This blend of theory and practice is designed to prepare managers for the realities of leading in a fast-paced, ever-changing business environment.

The author brings a wealth of experience and a diverse range of perspectives to this book. Their backgrounds in business leadership, organizational psychology, and strategic consulting enrich the content with depth and practicality. Through this book, they share not just their successes but also the lessons learned from challenges they have faced, making it a comprehensive resource for anyone looking to enhance their leadership skills.

As you delve into the chapters of this book, you will find yourself equipped to handle the complexities of modern management. Whether it's leveraging new technologies, managing remote teams, or fostering a culture of innovation, this book provides you with the insights and tools to lead effectively. It encourages you to reflect on your own leadership style, challenges you to think critically about your approach to management and inspires you to become a visionary leader who can confidently navigate the business maze.

We are confident that "Navigating the Business Maze: Essential Management Skills for Today's Leaders" will serve as an invaluable resource for managers across all levels and industries. Whether you are a seasoned executive seeking to refine your skills or a new manager stepping into your first leadership role, the lessons within these pages will empower you to make a significant impact on your organization and your career.

Welcome to a journey of transformation, where you will learn not only to manage but to lead with vision, integrity, and effectiveness. Let this book be your guide as you navigate the complexities of modern management and carve your path to becoming an exemplary leader.

Introduction

In the ever-evolving landscape of business, the role of a manager transcends traditional boundaries, weaving through complex challenges and pioneering new strategies for success. "Navigating the Business Maze: Essential Management Skills for Today's Leaders" is designed to equip current and aspiring managers with the critical skills needed to thrive in this dynamic environment.

This book delves into the core aspects of effective management, from foundational principles to the integration of cutting-edge technologies. Each chapter is crafted to address key components of management, offering insights into planning, organizing, leading, and controlling, with an emphasis on strategic decision-making and leadership development. By exploring these elements, the book aims to sculpt proficient leaders who can steer their organizations through the complexities of the modern business world.

Furthermore, "Navigating the Business Maze" is more than just a guide; it is a toolkit for transformation. It encourages managers to evolve from traditional roles and adopt innovative approaches to leadership and problem-solving. The book is replete with real-world examples, case studies, and practical tools that bring theoretical concepts to life, enabling readers to apply learned strategies effectively within their own teams and organizations.

As we progress through the chapters, readers will gain insights into adapting to changing business environments, leveraging technology for management, and developing essential leadership qualities. This comprehensive approach ensures that managers not only understand the responsibilities and challenges of their roles but are also prepared to anticipate and react strategically to the unpredictable twists and turns of the business world.

Embark on this journey through "Navigating the Business Maze" to transform your management style, enhance your leadership skills, and achieve unparalleled success in your professional endeavors. Whether you are a seasoned executive or a novice manager, this book will serve as an indispensable guide as you navigate the complex maze of modern business management.

"Management is doing things right; leadership is doing the right things."

— Peter Drucker

"The very essence of leadership is that you have to have a vision. It's got to be a vision you articulate clearly and forcefully on every occasion. You can't blow an uncertain trumpet."

— Theodore M. Hesburgh

"The function of leadership is to produce more leaders, not more followers."

— Ralph Nader

"Innovation distinguishes between a leader and a follower."

— Steve Jobs

"The greatest leader is not necessarily the one who does the greatest things. He is the one that gets the people to do the greatest things."

— Ronald Reagan

CHAPTER 1
The Foundations of Effective Management

Management serves as the fundamental pillar for any prosperous enterprise, guiding organizations in their pursuit of strategic goals. This chapter explores the core significance of management, emphasizing its crucial function in securing the success of businesses and scrutinizing the development of management theories that have molded current practices. Grasping these concepts enables managers to skillfully handle the intricacies of today's business landscape. By dissecting the journey of management thought and its impact on modern methodologies, this section provides a comprehensive overview of how management has evolved to meet the challenges of a dynamic and complex corporate world. Through a deeper understanding of these principles, managers are better equipped to lead their companies toward sustained success and adapt to the ever-changing demands of the business environment.

This chapter sets a robust foundation by detailing the fundamental principles of effective management and the evolving roles of managers in a modern context. As the business landscape continues to evolve, ongoing learning and self-assessment are vital. Managers are encouraged to reflect on their management style, identify areas for improvement, and continually seek new skills to enhance their effectiveness. This comprehensive approach ensures that managers are well-prepared to lead their organizations toward sustained success and adaptability in a dynamic business

Core Principles of Management and the Evolving Role of the Modern Manager

Effective management starts with robust planning. This involves setting clear, actionable objectives and crafting strategies that are not only comprehensive but anticipatory of future needs and challenges. A notable example of strategic planning is a tech startup that adeptly entered new markets by analysing market trends and customer needs, thus positioning itself advantageously in a competitive sector.

Organizing resources—people, capital, and materials—is pivotal in realizing a company's goals. For instance, a manufacturing firm that reorganized its operations demonstrated this principle by realigning its workforce and optimizing its supply chain, achieving a 20% increase in production without additional capital expenditure. This shows how an effective organization maximizes efficiency and output by ensuring that the right resources are deployed effectively.

Leadership is another critical facet of management. It involves motivating and directing staff to foster a productive and positive work environment. A practical example of leadership in action is a retail company that empowers its middle managers through a leadership development program. This initiative not only boosted employee satisfaction but also enhanced the company's performance by improving responsiveness to market dynamics.

The role of control involves monitoring the organization's progress toward its goals, including setting performance standards, measuring actual performance, and making necessary adjustments. A multinational corporation illustrated this by implementing a real-time data dashboard to monitor key performance indicators across different regions, leading to improved efficiencies globally.

Today's managers transcend traditional supervisory roles to become visionaries and strategists. The digital era demands that managers balance day-to-day administration with strategic foresight, often requiring them to be adaptable and innovative. A case in point is a manager in the fintech sector who led a project integrating artificial intelligence with traditional banking services, significantly enhancing customer service and operational efficiency.

Leadership and Adaptation in Changing Business Environments

While management ensures tasks are completed, leadership is about inspiring and motivating. Effective managers are also leaders who exhibit integrity, decisiveness, empathy, and resilience. For example, the leader of a non-profit organization transformed its approach, increasing volunteer engagement and expanding community impact, showcasing the power of effective leadership.

Adapting to change is crucial in today's fast-paced business world. This can be seen in how traditional businesses, like a publishing company that faced declining print sales, successfully transitioned to digital formats, thereby revitalizing its business model and expanding its market reach. Tools like agile management and scenario planning are instrumental in navigating through such significant changes and disruptions.

Technological Integration in Management

It is imperative for managers to incorporate cutting-edge tools to maintain a competitive edge. Technology significantly boosts managerial effectiveness through the utilization of various tools, such as data analytics, project management software, and digital communication platforms. For example, a logistics company that implemented Internet of Things (IoT) technology to monitor shipments in real-time experienced a substantial reduction in delays and a notable enhancement in customer satisfaction, showcasing the transformative impact technology can have on business operations.

Moreover, the integration of technology in management practices not only streamlines processes but also opens up new avenues for innovation and efficiency. Advanced analytical tools allow managers to make informed decisions by providing insights that were previously inaccessible, while project management software enhances collaboration and coordination among team members, regardless of their physical locations. Digital communication platforms facilitate instant communication and foster a more connected and responsive organizational environment. This digital transformation in management practices illustrates a paradigm shift in how businesses operate and compete in the modern marketplace. The strategic adoption of these technologies can lead to improved operational efficiencies, better customer engagement, and ultimately, greater business success.

CHAPTER 2
Leadership in Action

Cultivating Personal Leadership Styles and the Dynamics of Leading Diverse Teams

Leadership goes beyond ordinary management duties, acting as a foundational element for motivating individuals and guiding teams toward extraordinary accomplishments. This chapter delves deeply into the intricacies of leadership as it pertains to management, concentrating on cultivating personal leadership styles and proficiently managing heterogeneous teams. By enhancing your leadership strategy, you can foster a vibrant and encouraging workplace that is well-suited to meeting and exceeding organizational objectives.

Furthermore, this chapter explores how effective leadership is instrumental in shaping an organization's culture and driving it toward success. It emphasizes the importance of understanding the various leadership theories and applying them appropriately in diverse team settings. Through a detailed examination of different leadership models, this chapter assists managers in identifying the most suitable approaches that resonate with their personalities and organizational needs. By refining these methods, leaders are empowered to inspire trust and foster a sense of unity among team members, thereby enhancing overall productivity and achieving strategic goals.

Developing Effective Leadership Styles

Leadership styles, ranging from autocratic to democratic, each carry significant implications for team dynamics and overall organizational success. It's crucial for leaders to identify their inherent style and adapt it according to different situational needs—a concept known as situational leadership. This flexibility is vital for effectively tackling a variety of challenges and opportunities.

For example, consider the leadership transformation at NextGen Robotics, a leading firm in automation technology. The CEO, originally favoring an autocratic style, shifted to a more democratic approach as the company scaled. This transition was strategic, aiming to foster a culture of innovation. By encouraging team input in decision-making processes, NextGen saw a notable increase in innovative solutions and employee satisfaction, illustrating the impact of adaptive leadership styles on a company's growth and adaptability.

Cultivating a Cohesive and Inclusive Team Environment

Managing diverse teams effectively requires an in-depth understanding of diversity, which includes navigating cultural, educational, and generational differences. Implementing inclusive strategies ensures clear communication and fosters a collaborative team environment. Additionally, managing conflicts constructively is critical to maintaining team cohesion.

A practical example can be seen at Global Tech Solutions, a multinational IT service provider. The company faced challenges with team cohesion across its culturally diverse workforce. By introducing cultural sensitivity training and regular team-building retreats, Global Tech successfully enhanced understanding and cooperation among its team members, leading to improved project outcomes and a stronger, more inclusive company culture.

Enhancing Motivation and Engagement

Understanding what motivates individuals is key to enhancing team performance. Managers can apply motivational theories strategically to set appropriate goals and recognize achievements, boosting team morale and productivity. Furthermore, fostering a culture of trust and loyalty is crucial; this involves transparency, showing appreciation for team efforts, and providing professional development opportunities.

For instance, at Harmony Health, a healthcare startup, the management implemented a tailored motivation strategy that included transparent communication about company goals, a robust recognition program, and opportunities for career advancement. This approach not only motivated the team but also significantly reduced turnover rates, showcasing the importance of aligning motivational strategies with employee needs for optimal results.

Navigating Modern Leadership Challenges

Today's leaders face unique challenges, including navigating organizational changes, managing remote or hybrid teams, and maintaining ethical standards under pressure. Leaders must be adept at guiding their teams through these challenges effectively, ensuring integrity and productivity.

A relevant case study involves RemoteComms, a communications firm that transitioned to a fully remote operation amid growing global challenges. The leadership team developed a comprehensive remote work policy that included regular virtual check-ins, clear communication protocols, and digital tools for collaboration and project management. This strategic approach helped maintain team unity and high performance despite the shift in work dynamics.

Effective leadership is a dynamic skill requiring ongoing learning and adaptation. This chapter has provided insights into developing a leadership style that is personal and impactful, along with strategies for leading diverse and high-performing teams. Leaders committed to continual improvement and adaptability can inspire their teams to achieve remarkable results, effectively navigating the complex landscape of modern management. The insights and case studies presented illustrate how versatile and responsive leadership can lead to sustained success and organizational resilience.

CHAPTER 3
Strategic Decision-Making

Techniques for Making Informed Decisions that Steer the Company towards Long-term Success

Strategic decision-making stands as a critical skill for leaders striving to steer their organizations toward ongoing viability and prosperity. This chapter delves deeply into the crucial methodologies and insights necessary for executing informed and impactful decisions. By mastering these strategic approaches, managers can expertly maneuver through the complexities of the business landscape, guaranteeing that their decisions are not only proactive but also thoroughly aligned with the specific needs of their organizations.

In addition, this chapter explores the frameworks and tools that enhance decision-making processes, providing leaders with the ability to anticipate future challenges and opportunities. By integrating advanced analytical techniques and adopting a forward-thinking mindset, leaders can craft strategies that foster long-term growth and stability. This comprehensive examination helps managers develop a robust understanding of strategic decision-making, equipping them with the skills to make decisions that effectively respond to both current and future business demands.

Strategic Decision-Making: Concepts and Frameworks

Strategic decision-making is about evaluating information from multiple sources, considering long-term outcomes, and ensuring that decisions contribute to a sustainable competitive advantage. It involves distinguishing between strategic, tactical, and operational decisions and understanding how each plays a role in the broader vision of the organization.

To facilitate sound strategic decision-making, several analytical frameworks are invaluable. The SWOT analysis helps identify internal Strengths and Weaknesses, along with external Opportunities and Threats. PESTLE analysis expands this by analyzing Political, Economic, Social, Technological, Legal, and Environmental factors that affect the organization. Another critical tool, Porter's Five Forces, provides insights into the competitive environment and market dynamics. For example, a tech startup may use these frameworks to decide on a new market entry strategy, evaluating not only its internal capabilities but also the external competitive landscape and regulatory environment.

Leveraging Data in Strategic Decision-Making

In the contemporary digital landscape, data analytics has emerged as a foundational element of strategic decision-making. This section underscores the critical role of data in comprehending market trends, consumer behaviors, and operational efficiencies. By harnessing the power of big data, artificial intelligence, and machine learning, leaders are equipped to make decisions grounded in evidence, which not only minimize risks but also optimize opportunities for growth and profit.

Consider the example of a retail chain that utilizes data analytics to monitor customer purchasing behaviors. By analyzing this data, the chain can adeptly adjust inventory levels, ensuring they align with actual consumer demand. This strategic use of data significantly diminishes waste and enhances profitability by preventing overstocking and understocking scenarios. Furthermore, this approach allows the retailer to respond more dynamically to market changes, tailor promotions and product placements that resonate with customer preferences, and ultimately drive increased customer satisfaction and loyalty. This segment illustrates how integrating data analytics into business operations can transform insights into actionable strategies that lead to tangible business outcomes.

Balancing Intuition and Analytics

While the importance of data is undeniable in today's business landscape, the value of intuition—rooted in a leader's experience and knowledge—continues to hold significant relevance. Managers who can effectively balance analytical thinking with instinctive insights are better equipped to adopt a comprehensive approach to decision-making. This balanced method enables leaders to utilize the best of both worlds: the precision of data-driven decisions and the nuanced understanding that comes from experiential knowledge.

For example, consider a seasoned CEO who leverages her intuition, honed over years of leadership, to make a crucial decision regarding the acquisition of a competitor. This intuitive decision is not made in isolation but is complemented by rigorous data analysis to confirm the viability and strategic advantage of the acquisition. The CEO's deep industry knowledge and firsthand experiences provide a unique perspective that data alone might not reveal, while the data provides a solid foundation of facts and figures to support her intuitive insights. This integration of intuition and data ensures that the decision is both strategically sound and deeply informed, optimizing the chances of a successful outcome.

Implementing and Monitoring Strategic Decisions

The effectiveness of strategic decisions hinges on their implementation. This section outlines best practices for rolling out decisions within an organization, including setting clear timelines, allocating resources efficiently, and defining metrics for success. Additionally, it underscores the importance of monitoring the outcomes and making necessary adjustments to stay on track with organizational goals. A practical example is a manufacturing company that implemented a new operational strategy to increase efficiency; by closely monitoring performance metrics, the company was able to make iterative improvements that significantly boosted production output.

Ethical Considerations in Strategic Decision-Making

Strategic decisions often involve significant ethical considerations. Leaders must ensure their choices not only advance corporate goals but also uphold ethical standards and contribute positively to the community and environment. This section discusses how to navigate complex ethical dilemmas and make decisions that reflect corporate social responsibility. An example here could be a company deciding against outsourcing labor to regions with less stringent labor laws, even if it would be more cost-effective, prioritizing ethical practices over lower operational costs.

Strategic decision-making is an iterative process that necessitates a nuanced balance of analytical prowess, intuitive understanding, and ethical deliberation. By adopting the frameworks and methodologies outlined in this chapter, leaders are equipped to make well-informed decisions that drive their organizations toward enduring success and adaptability. These decisions are not only based on solid data and personal insights but are also framed within ethical guidelines, ensuring that each choice supports sustainable and responsible business practices.

The forthcoming chapter will delve into the mastery of communication, a pivotal skill set for effective management.

It will highlight various strategies to enhance the clarity and effectiveness of communication within an organization. This exploration will address the importance of clear communication in fostering an engaged and collaborative workplace, which is crucial for implementing strategic decisions and maintaining organizational harmony. Through improved communication skills, leaders can ensure that their strategic visions are understood and embraced across all levels of the organization, further enhancing their ability to lead effectively.

Timothy O. Enitinwa

CHAPTER 4
Communication Mastery

Tools for Enhancing Clarity and Efficiency in Internal and External Communications

Effective communication is fundamental to successful management, acting as the crucial link that transforms ambiguity into clarity. It cultivates an environment rich in understanding and collaboration, essential for both internal operations and external engagements. This chapter delves into mastering the art of communication, offering an array of tools and strategies designed to augment clarity and efficiency across various business interactions.

Through practical examples and case studies, the chapter outlines methods for enhancing verbal, written, and non-verbal communication. It emphasizes the importance of active listening, clear messaging, and the tailored delivery of information to diverse audiences. These skills are indispensable for leaders seeking to motivate teams, negotiate with partners, and maintain transparent relationships with stakeholders. By applying these communication strategies, managers can effectively navigate complex dialogues and foster a cooperative atmosphere that promotes shared goals and mutual success.

The Importance of Clear Communication

In the realm of business, communication is multifaceted, ranging from daily interactions with team members to complex negotiations with external partners. Clear communication is critical for achieving business objectives, enhancing team cohesion, and building strong relationships with stakeholders. Miscommunication can lead to errors, misunderstandings, and inefficiencies, ultimately impacting the bottom line. For instance, a multinational corporation experienced significant project delays due to miscommunication between its cross-continental teams. By implementing a standardized communication protocol, the company saw a marked improvement in project delivery times and reduced miscommunications.

Developing Effective Communication Skills

Listening Skills: Active listening is foundational to effective communication. This section underscores the importance of listening to understand—not merely to respond. Techniques such as reflective listening, where managers repeat back what they have heard to confirm understanding, can enhance listening abilities significantly.

Verbal and Non-Verbal Communication: This segment covers the nuances of verbal expressions and the significant impact of non-verbal cues, such as body language and tone of voice, on the perception of the message conveyed. Effective leaders must be adept at both expressing themselves clearly and reading the non-verbal cues of others. A practical example could be a manager who adjusted his body language during presentations, which led to increased engagement and more positive feedback from the team.

Writing Skills: In today's digital age, strong writing skills are indispensable. This part provides guidelines for crafting clear, concise, and professional emails, reports, and proposals. For example, a team leader at a tech firm developed a template for reporting that simplified the communication of complex information, making it easier for different departments to quickly grasp key points and take action.

Communicating Across Cultures

With global operations, the ability to communicate across cultural boundaries is more crucial than ever. This section explores the challenges and strategies for effective cross-cultural communication, including understanding cultural norms, avoiding cultural faux pas, and adapting communication styles to diverse audiences. An effective strategy employed by an international consultancy firm involved training sessions on cultural nuances that enabled their managers to handle negotiations and team management more effectively in different cultural settings.

Leveraging Technology in Communication

Technology has transformed how businesses communicate. This section reviews current tools and platforms that enhance interaction efficiency, such as collaborative software, instant messaging apps, and video conferencing tools. It also discusses future trends in communication technology that managers need to be aware of. For instance, the introduction of AI-driven communication tools in a marketing firm allowed for real-time customer service responses, significantly improving customer satisfaction rates.

Crisis Communication

Handling communication during a crisis is a vital competency for any manager. This section articulates the principles of effective crisis communication, emphasizing the importance of being transparent, responsive, and consistent. It offers a detailed step-by-step guide on how to prepare and execute a communication plan when a crisis strikes, ensuring that managers can effectively manage the situation and mitigate potential damage.

To illustrate these principles in action, consider the case study of a fictional company, "GreenTech Innovations," which faced allegations of environmental violations at one of its manufacturing plants. As news of the allegations spread, it threatened to tarnish GreenTech's reputation as a leader in environmentally friendly technology.

In response, GreenTech's management team acted swiftly, issuing a public statement within hours of the allegations surfacing. This initial response emphasized their commitment to maintaining the highest environmental standards and announced an immediate internal investigation to address the concerns raised. Throughout the crisis, GreenTech provided regular updates through various channels, including social media, press releases, and its corporate website, maintaining transparency with all stakeholders.

Additionally, GreenTech set up a dedicated hotline and email service to handle inquiries, ensuring that responses were timely and that the public could engage directly with the company during this critical time. They also organized a press conference where the CEO personally addressed the media, outlining the steps the company was taking and reaffirming its commitment to environmental responsibility.

The investigation eventually revealed that the supposed violations were due to a misunderstanding related to waste disposal procedures. GreenTech took corrective action by revising its waste management protocols and conducting comprehensive training for their employees to prevent future incidents. They also hosted community forums to discuss their commitment to environmental standards, further demonstrating their dedication to transparency and accountability.

This case highlights the importance of a rapid and coordinated response in managing a crisis. By adhering to the principles of transparency, responsiveness, and consistency in their communication, GreenTech was able to mitigate the damage to its reputation, regain public trust, and emerge from the crisis stronger, with improved operational protocols that underscored their commitment to continuous improvement and environmental stewardship.

By following the outlined approach, managers can develop the skills necessary to lead their teams through challenging times with confidence and integrity, ensuring that transparency, responsiveness, and consistent messaging preserve trust and stability within the organization and with the public.

Training and Development for Communication Skills

Recognizing that communication skills develop over time, this part suggests methods for ongoing improvement, including training programs, workshops, and personal coaching. It highlights the value of continuous learning and feedback in refining communication abilities. An annual retreat focused on communication excellence could be a practical example, where managers participate in advanced communication workshops and receive feedback on their communication styles.

Mastering communication is an essential, ongoing journey for any leader. This chapter has equipped readers with the tools and knowledge to enhance their communication skills, thereby improving their management effectiveness. Effective communication not only clarifies tasks and expectations but also builds stronger relationships, paving the way for business success. The next chapter will explore financial acumen for managers, delving into the basic financial management skills necessary for non-financial leaders to make informed decisions.

CHAPTER 5
Financial Acumen for Managers

Basic Financial Management Skills Necessary for Non-Financial Leaders

Financial acumen is increasingly recognized as an indispensable skill for managers at all levels, extending well beyond traditional finance roles to become a core component of effective leadership. This chapter focuses on equipping non-financial managers with the essential financial knowledge and tools they need to make informed decisions that can significantly enhance their organization's bottom line and contribute to its overall financial health and strategic objectives.

Understanding key financial concepts such as budgeting, forecasting, profit and loss, and cash flow management allows managers to interpret financial reports, understand the financial implications of their decisions, and communicate more effectively with finance professionals. Moreover, this knowledge empowers them to identify potential financial opportunities and risks, ensuring that their decisions are aligned with the organization's long-term goals.

By providing non-financial managers with a solid foundation in financial principles, this chapter helps them to contribute more effectively to their organization's success. It emphasizes practical applications and real-world examples, giving managers the tools they need to apply financial concepts directly to their operational responsibilities. Whether it's planning a new project, managing departmental budgets, or assessing the financial viability of a new product line, these skills are crucial for leading teams and driving the organization forward.

Understanding Financial Statements

Balance Sheets: The balance sheet provides a snapshot of a company's assets, liabilities, and equity at a specific point in time, which is essential for assessing organizational health and financial stability. For example, a project manager might use the balance sheet to determine the company's capacity to fund a new project without jeopardizing financial stability.

Income Statements: Also known as the profit and loss statement, the income statement shows a company's revenues, expenses, and profits over a specific period, which is crucial for evaluating operational efficiency and profitability. A marketing manager would find this valuable to gauge how their campaigns affect the company's overall profitability.

Cash Flow Statements: Understanding the flow of cash in and out of the business through the cash flow statement is vital to ensuring the business maintains adequate liquidity for operations. Facilities managers might use this information to schedule significant upgrades or maintenance, aligning these expenses with cash availability.

Budgeting and Forecasting

Budgeting and forecasting are critical financial management skills that enable organizations to plan and control their financial resources effectively, ensuring alignment with business goals and anticipated financial conditions. These practices serve as a roadmap, guiding financial decision-making and resource allocation across various departments.

An example of how these skills are applied can be seen in the role of an HR manager. In managing hiring initiatives, an HR manager must align recruitment strategies with the organization's financial forecasts and overall business needs. This involves creating accurate budgets for recruitment activities, such as advertising job openings, conducting interviews, and onboarding new employees. The HR manager uses forecasting to predict future hiring needs based on business growth projections, seasonal fluctuations in business activities, and turnover rates.

By integrating budgeting and forecasting into the recruitment process, the HR manager ensures that hiring plans are financially viable and contribute to the strategic objectives of the organization. This alignment helps prevent overstaffing or understaffing scenarios, which can lead to unnecessary expenses or operational challenges, respectively. Through effective budgeting and forecasting, organizations can optimize their financial resources and maintain a workforce that is well-suited to their current and future business requirements.

Financial Decision-Making

Cost-Benefit Analysis: Managers often need to perform cost-benefit analyses to make informed business decisions. Learning how to weigh the costs and benefits of various options helps managers choose initiatives that offer the greatest return on investment, such as selecting between different technologies solutions to improve productivity.

Investment Appraisal Techniques: Familiarity with investment appraisal techniques like ROI (Return on Investment), NPV (Net Present Value), and IRR (Internal Rate of Return) is critical for evaluating potential investments and making strategic business decisions. An operations manager, for example, might apply these techniques to assess the feasibility of investing in new manufacturing equipment.

Managing Financial Risks

Strategies to identify, analyze, and mitigate financial risks is crucial for safeguarding a company's assets and earning potential. Consider a supply chain manager who employs risk management techniques to evaluate supplier reliability and mitigate risks associated with supply chain disruptions.

Communicating Financial Information

Non-financial managers must be skilled at communicating financial information to various stakeholders, including staff, senior management, and external parties. Effective communication involves presenting financial data clearly and understandably, such as a department head explaining budget variances to non-financial senior executives using simplified charts and key financial indicators.

Financial acumen is a key competency for all managers, not just those in accounting or finance. This chapter has provided a foundational understanding of financial principles and practical tools for non-financial managers. By integrating these skills into their management practices, leaders can significantly enhance their contributions to their organization's financial health and strategic success. The next chapter will explore the integration of technology in management, demonstrating how modern tools can enhance managerial effectiveness.

CHAPTER 6
Innovation and Change Management

Strategies for Fostering Innovation and Managing Change within the Organization

The ability to innovate and effectively manage change is critical for an organization's survival and growth. This chapter offers practical strategies for fostering an environment that encourages innovation and outlines successful methodologies for managing organizational change. By mastering these concepts, managers are better equipped to guide their teams through transitions smoothly and sustain a competitive edge in the market.

The chapter begins by exploring how to cultivate a culture of innovation within an organization. This includes encouraging creativity, supporting risk-taking, and implementing systems that reward innovative ideas. It highlights the importance of leadership in setting the tone for innovation and how managers can act as catalysts for change by championing and modeling innovative behaviors.

Additionally, the chapter delves into the complexities of managing organizational change. It discusses the stages of change management, from planning and communication to implementation and evaluation. Strategies such as engaging stakeholders, maintaining open lines of communication, and providing training and support are emphasized to ensure successful change initiatives. By providing managers with the tools to create an innovative environment and manage change effectively, this chapter helps leaders not only adapt to changes but also drive them, thereby ensuring their organization remains relevant and competitive in an ever-evolving marketplace.

Cultivating an Innovative Environment

Encouraging Creativity: Fostering a workplace culture that values creativity and open-mindedness is the first step toward innovation. Encouraging team members to think outside the box and rewarding innovative ideas are critical.

Implementing regular brainstorming sessions and creative workshops can stimulate creative thinking. For example, a tech company introduced 'Innovation Fridays,' where team members could work on any project they were passionate about, leading to the development of new product ideas.

Resource Allocation for Innovation: Innovation requires a dedicated investment of time, capital, and resources. Allocating specific resources for innovation projects, such as funding for research and development and technology upgrades, is essential. A notable example is a pharmaceutical company that allocated 15% of its budget to R&D, significantly enhancing its capability to bring new drugs to market faster than its competitors.

Collaborative Innovation: The benefits of collaborative innovation, both within the organization and with external partners, are immense. Encouraging cross-departmental collaborations and forming partnerships with academic institutions, startups, or other businesses can enhance innovative capabilities. A case in point involves a consumer electronics firm that partnered with a university research lab, leading to breakthroughs in battery technology.

Managing Organizational Change

Understanding Change Dynamics: Recognizing the typical stages of change within an organization and the common emotional responses among employees helps managers anticipate and mitigate resistance to change. Familiarizing oneself with these dynamics is foundational for facilitating smooth transitions.

Strategies for Effective Change Management: Introducing proven change management models and frameworks, such as Kotter's 8-Step Process for Leading Change or the ADKAR model, can guide successful change initiatives. For instance, a retail chain implemented Kotter's model to restructure its customer service operations, resulting in improved customer satisfaction scores.

Communication During Change: The role of communication in the change management process is critical. Clear, transparent, and continuous communication strategies provide all stakeholders with timely updates about the change process and its benefits, ensuring alignment and reducing uncertainties.

Leveraging Technology in Change Management

Various technologies can significantly enhance change management efforts, providing tools that streamline processes and improve the precision of monitoring and reporting. Technologies such as project management software, digital communication platforms, and data analytics tools are instrumental in facilitating smooth transitions and effective change management.

For instance, consider a logistics company facing a major operational shift. By employing advanced project management software, the company was able to improve task coordination and ensure strict adherence to deadlines. This technology provided a centralized platform for managing all aspects of the change, from initial planning and scheduling to execution and follow-up. The software enabled real-time updates and communication among team members, ensuring that everyone was on the same page and could adjust to new tasks and timelines quickly. Moreover, digital communication platforms facilitate seamless interactions among diverse teams, significant in large-scale operations that may involve multiple departments or geographical locations. These platforms ensured that communication barriers did not hinder the change process, allowing for immediate feedback and collaborative problem-solving.

Additionally, data analytics tools played a crucial role in measuring the effectiveness of the change initiatives. These tools helped the company track performance metrics closely, providing insights into areas of success and those needing improvement. By analyzing data generated during the transition, managers could make informed decisions, fine-tune processes, and ensure that the operational shift aligned with strategic objectives. Through the integration of these technologies, the logistics company not only managed the change more efficiently but also minimized disruption to its operations, ultimately leading to enhanced organizational performance and customer satisfaction.

Overcoming Barriers to Innovation and Change

Identifying and Addressing Barriers: Common barriers to innovation and change include cultural resistance, limited resources, and a lack of leadership support. Developing strategies to identify and overcome these barriers is crucial for the successful implementation of new ideas and changes. A detailed discussion might include strategies such as leadership training to enhance support for innovation initiatives. Case studies of successful innovation and change management initiatives highlight the strategies used and the outcomes achieved. These real-life examples provide inspiration and guidance for managers facing similar challenges, such as a telecommunications company that successfully navigated a digital transformation by overhauling its IT infrastructure and training its workforce in new digital skills.

Innovation and change management are essential components of a modern business strategy. This chapter has equipped managers with the tools and knowledge needed to foster an innovative atmosphere and manage change effectively. By applying these strategies, managers can lead their organizations toward sustained growth and adaptability in an ever-changing business environment. The subsequent chapter will delve into building high-performance teams, outlining techniques for recruiting, motivating, and retaining top talent.

Timothy O. Enitinwa

CHAPTER 7
Building High-Performance Teams

How to Recruit, Motivate, and Retain the Best Talent

Building high-performance teams is crucial for achieving organizational goals and securing a competitive advantage. In today's dynamic business environment, the ability to assemble, lead, and maintain teams composed of the best talent is not just advantageous— it's essential for success. This chapter delves into the nuanced strategies and practices necessary for recruiting, motivating, and retaining top-tier talent. By mastering these elements, managers can forge teams that are not only skilled and diverse but also deeply committed and highly productive. Understanding how to effectively blend individual talents into a cohesive unit that excels in achieving set objectives is a key focus of this discussion.

Recruiting the Right Talent

Defining Team Needs: Successful recruitment begins with a clear understanding of the team's needs. Conducting a thorough job analysis to identify the key competencies and attributes needed aligns recruitment efforts with the team's and organization's strategic goals. For example, a technology startup may prioritize agility and technical expertise to support rapid product development cycles.

Effective Recruitment Strategies: Utilizing a variety of recruitment techniques—from traditional job postings to more innovative approaches like social media recruiting and employee referrals—is crucial. Emphasizing a transparent and inclusive hiring process attracts a diverse pool of candidates, enriching the organization's cultural and intellectual fabric.

Assessing Candidates: Implementing best practices in candidate evaluation is critical. This includes structured interviews, skill assessments, and personality tests to ensure that a candidate's values align with the company culture, promoting a long-term fit. For instance, a firm might use behavioral assessment tools to predict how well candidates will integrate into existing teams.

Motivating Team Members

Understanding Motivation: Managers must grasp various motivational theories, such as Maslow's hierarchy of needs and Herzberg's two-factor theory, to tailor motivation strategies effectively. This understanding helps in creating specific incentives and work environments that foster high levels of employee motivation.

Creating a Motivating Environment: Developing a work environment that promotes motivation through meaningful work, recognition, and career development opportunities is essential. Leadership plays a pivotal role in setting a motivational tone, with managers acting as role models. An example here could be a manager who regularly sets aside time to recognize individual and team achievements, significantly boosting morale.

Employee Engagement Techniques: Techniques to increase employee engagement include setting clear goals, providing regular feedback, and involving team members in decision-making processes. These practices not only motivate but also empower employees, leading to higher job satisfaction and productivity.

Retaining Talent

The Importance of Retention: Understanding the high costs associated with turnover and the significant benefits of retaining top talent is fundamental. Effective retention strategies begin with a deep understanding of why employees stay and why they might leave.

Retention Strategies: Offering competitive compensation packages, comprehensive benefits, work-life balance initiatives, and continuous learning opportunities are effective retention strategies. Additionally, career pathing and succession planning are crucial for long-term employee engagement and satisfaction.

Building a Supportive Culture: The role of organizational culture in retention cannot be overstated. A supportive, inclusive, and respectful workplace culture significantly enhances employee satisfaction and loyalty. For example, a company that actively promotes an open and inclusive culture may experience lower turnover rates and higher employee engagement.

Leveraging Team Diversity

Leveraging the diversity of a team offers numerous advantages that can significantly enhance organizational performance. A diverse team brings increased creativity, improved problem-solving capabilities, and a broader range of perspectives, all of which contribute to stronger performance and better business outcomes. The varied backgrounds and experiences of team members lead to a richer pool of ideas, fostering innovation and enabling the organization to address complex challenges more effectively.

Effectively managing diverse teams involves several crucial strategies to ensure that every team member feels valued and included. Addressing communication barriers and cultural sensitivities is essential. Implementing inclusion strategies, such as training programs focused on cultural competency, is also vital. These programs help team members understand and appreciate the different backgrounds and perspectives within the team. Additionally, regular team-building activities are designed to enhance mutual understanding and respect among team members. These activities not only improve interpersonal relationships but also strengthen the team's ability to work effectively together, ensuring that the benefits of diversity are fully realized.

Building high-performance teams involves more than just assembling a group of talented individuals; it requires creating a cohesive unit that shares a common purpose and collective goals. This chapter has provided comprehensive strategies for recruiting, motivating, and retaining employees—essential components for forming and maintaining successful teams. By applying these principles, managers can cultivate an environment where team members are not only satisfied but also highly productive. The next chapter will focus on conflict resolution and negotiation, crucial skills for maintaining harmony and achieving optimal team performance.

CHAPTER 8
Conflict Resolution and Negotiation

Effective Methods for Resolving Disputes and Negotiating Favourable Outcomes

Conflict and negotiation are integral aspects of management that, when managed adeptly, can prevent minor disagreements from escalating into significant issues and transform negotiations into opportunities for organizational growth. This chapter explores essential strategies for conflict resolution and negotiation, providing managers with the tools needed to navigate disputes constructively and secure favourable outcomes. Mastering the skills of conflict resolution involves understanding the underlying causes of disagreements and addressing them in a way that respects all parties involved. Effective conflict management not only prevents disruptions but also enhances team cohesion and trust. On the other hand, negotiation skills are crucial for reaching agreements that satisfy all parties' needs and advance the organization's objectives. This includes preparing thoroughly, communicating clearly, and employing tactics that foster mutual benefit.

By equipping managers with these critical skills, the chapter aims to help maintain a harmonious work environment and achieve strategic objectives. Effective conflict resolution and negotiation lead to stronger relationships within the organization, promoting an atmosphere of cooperation and mutual respect. Ultimately, these capabilities are vital for any leader seeking to enhance organizational performance and drive growth.

Understanding and Addressing Conflict

Identifying the types of conflicts that can arise in the workplace is crucial—be it interpersonal, team, or organizational conflicts. Each type of conflict requires a tailored approach to resolution, starting with a clear understanding of its nature and underlying causes. Common causes include communication barriers, personality clashes, power struggles, and conflicts over resource allocation.

Recognizing these causes is the first step in developing effective strategies to address them.

Effective communication is central to resolving conflicts. Techniques such as active listening, which involves fully concentrating on what is being said rather than passively hearing the message, empathetic responses, and clear, assertive communication are vital. These methods help de-escalate tensions and foster an environment where mutual understanding can thrive. Moreover, problem-solving approaches that focus on finding a win-win solution are critical. Strategies like identifying common goals and brainstorming solutions together encourage collaboration and can lead to mutually beneficial outcomes. In some cases, third-party intervention through mediation or facilitation might be necessary to help resolve disputes that parties cannot handle independently.

Mastering Negotiation Techniques

Effective negotiation requires thorough preparation and planning. Understanding the interests of all parties involved and setting clear objectives are foundational elements. Managers must also be skilled in basic negotiation techniques, such as using open-ended questions to encourage dialogue, understanding the importance of making concessions, and mastering techniques for effectively closing negotiations.

Ethical considerations play a pivotal role in negotiations. Ensuring that all parties are treated fairly and that agreements are sustainable and enforceable is essential for maintaining trust and integrity within professional relationships. Ethical negotiations prioritize transparency and seek to avoid exploitation, aiming instead to achieve outcomes that are equitable and beneficial for all involved.

Practical Application and Continuous Learning

To bring these concepts to life, the chapter includes case studies that illustrate successful conflict resolution and negotiation scenarios. These real-life examples provide practical insights and demonstrate the application of theoretical concepts in various settings. For instance, a case study might detail how a manager successfully navigated a high-stakes contract negotiation by employing these techniques, resulting in a profitable deal that also strengthened long-term business relationships.

Encouraging ongoing development of these skills is crucial. Managers should engage in training sessions, workshops, and practical experiences to refine their abilities in conflict resolution and negotiation. Continuous learning is key to mastering these complex interpersonal skills and staying effective in evolving business environments.

By mastering conflict resolution and negotiation, managers can enhance team cohesion, improve organizational outcomes, and build stronger relationships both within and outside the organization. This chapter provides managers with a comprehensive toolkit to handle conflicts constructively and negotiate effectively, paving the way for enhanced organizational performance and growth. The subsequent chapter will explore ethics and corporate responsibility, delving into how managers can integrate ethical decision-making into their leadership practices to further enrich their professional environment and societal contributions.

Timothy O. Enitinwa

CHAPTER 9
Ethics and Corporate Responsibility

Guiding Principles for Ethical Decision-Making and Promoting Corporate Social Responsibility

In today's business environment, ethics and corporate responsibility transcend mere compliance—they are fundamental pillars of sustainable success and key to earning public trust. This chapter explores the crucial roles of ethical leadership and corporate social responsibility (CSR) in shaping a business that not only thrives but also positively impacts society. Through detailed frameworks and strategies, managers are equipped to ensure that their decisions uphold the highest ethical standards and effectively integrate CSR into their business practices.

Ethical Leadership: Defining and Benefiting from Integrity and Accountability

Ethical leadership is defined by key characteristics such as integrity, accountability, fairness, and respect for others. Embracing these traits not only guides leaders in making morally sound decisions but also fosters a culture that promotes long-term organizational success. The benefits of ethical leadership are profound, ranging from an enhanced reputation to increased trust among stakeholders, which are crucial for a supportive and sustainable business environment.

For instance, consider a technology firm that placed a strong emphasis on transparent communication and ethical practices in its operations. By prioritizing these values, the firm not only successfully avoided legal pitfalls but also enhanced its attractiveness to both investors and potential talent. This approach demonstrated the tangible benefits of ethical leadership. Investors are often drawn to companies that exhibit a strong commitment to ethics and transparency, as these qualities can significantly reduce the risks associated with governance and compliance. Similarly, top talent is increasingly seeking employment with organizations known for their ethical standards, as these environments are viewed as more supportive and sustainable. Consequently, the firm's dedication to ethical practices not only safeguarded its operations but also contributed to its competitive advantage in the marketplace, attracting both financial backing and skilled professionals.

Principles of Ethical Decision-Making

Adopting structured frameworks aids ethical decision-making. Models such as the Utilitarian Approach, which focuses on the greatest good for the greatest number, and the Virtue Approach, which emphasizes moral character, are instrumental in guiding leaders. These frameworks help ensure decisions are not just legally compliant but are also morally commendable.

Managers often face complex ethical dilemmas where the right course of action is not always clear. In such situations, maintaining transparency and seeking counsel are vital steps in navigating these challenges responsibly. For instance, a manager at a manufacturing company may face a dilemma about environmental compliance; consulting industry experts and adhering to ethical decision-making models can guide the manager to a decision that balances business goals with environmental responsibility.

Corporate Social Responsibility: Integrating CSR into Business Strategy

Understanding and implementing CSR is crucial for modern businesses. CSR extends beyond environmental stewardship to include social equity and economic development, offering a holistic approach to business operations that benefits both society and the company. Practical advice on developing and executing effective CSR programs ensures that these initiatives align with business objectives and stakeholder expectations.

Successful CSR initiatives, such as a retail chain that sources sustainably and pays fair wages, not only enhance brand reputation but also contribute to economic development by setting industry standards that encourage similar practices across the board.

Building a Culture of Ethics and Responsibility

Creating an ethical workplace involves more than establishing a code of ethics; it requires regular training on ethical practices and systems for anonymous reporting of unethical behavior. This fosters a culture where ethical decision-making is the norm, not the exception. Engaging stakeholders effectively in discussions about ethical practices and CSR initiatives is essential for transparency and trust. For example, a multinational corporation may hold quarterly forums with stakeholders to report on CSR progress and gather feedback, ensuring alignment with community and investor expectations.

Ethical Challenges in the Global Marketplace

Navigating ethical standards in a global business environment presents a set of unique challenges, particularly when dealing with diverse cultural norms, legal standards, and business practices. Companies operating internationally must find a balance between respecting local customs and maintaining their core ethical principles, a task that requires both sensitivity and firmness.

One effective strategy for managing these challenges is to adapt ethical standards to local contexts without compromising on core principles. This approach involves understanding and integrating into the local cultural and legal landscape while ensuring that the company's fundamental ethical commitments are not diluted. For instance, while gift-giving might be a customary practice in some cultures, companies must set clear guidelines to ensure that such practices do not conflict with their anti-corruption policies.

Furthermore, ensuring global consistency in ethical practices is crucial. This can be achieved through comprehensive training programs that educate all employees, regardless of location, about the company's ethical policies and the reasons behind them. Regular audits and reviews can also help ensure that these standards are being applied uniformly across all operations, helping to maintain a cohesive ethical stance throughout the organization. By adopting these strategies, businesses can uphold their ethical integrity while effectively navigating the complexities of the global marketplace.

Ethical leadership and corporate responsibility are about making a positive impact on society while building a sustainable business. This chapter has equipped managers with the necessary tools and knowledge to lead with integrity and foster a culture of responsibility. As businesses prepare for future challenges, the principles discussed here will be crucial in guiding ethical and responsible business practices that not only avoid negative consequences but actively contribute to societal well-being. The subsequent chapter will delve into future-proofing your business, highlighting the importance of continuous learning and adaptation in an ever-evolving business landscape.

CHAPTER 10
Future-Proofing Your Business

Preparing for Future Challenges through Continuous Learning and Adaptation

The concept of future-proofing your organization is crucial for sustained success. This chapter explores comprehensive strategies for preparing organizations to face future challenges and seize opportunities through a commitment to continuous learning, innovation, and adaptation. Embracing these elements enables managers to ensure their businesses are not only competitive but also resilient in the face of rapid change. By fostering a culture that prioritizes agility and proactive change management, businesses can navigate the uncertainties of tomorrow with confidence.

Embracing Technological Advancements and Continuous Learning

Staying Ahead with Technology: In the digital age, keeping pace with technological advancements is essential. Technologies such as artificial intelligence, machine learning, and blockchain are reshaping industries by transforming business operations and customer interactions. For example, a retail company implementing AI can personalize customer experiences, leading to increased loyalty and sales.

Implementing New Technologies: Successfully adopting new technologies involves more than just selection and acquisition. It requires a strategic approach that includes pilot testing, comprehensive staff training, and seamless integration into existing processes. This ensures that technological investments are maximized and truly beneficial to the business.

Cultivating a Culture of Continuous Learning: Establishing a workplace where continuous learning is valued is fundamental. Encouraging employee development through workshops, seminars, online courses, and cross-training opportunities equips staff with the skills necessary to adapt to new technologies and methodologies. For instance, a company might implement a learning management system that offers courses on emerging technologies and industry trends, keeping the workforce informed and skilled.

Adapting to Market Conditions and Promoting Innovation

Flexibility in Business Models: The ability to adapt business models in response to changing market demands is a significant aspect of future-proofing. This might involve diversifying product lines, exploring new markets, or adjusting service offerings in response to consumer behavior and market conditions.

Strategic Planning for Uncertainty: Employing techniques such as scenario planning and stress testing helps businesses prepare for various future scenarios. These tools enable companies to anticipate potential changes and develop adaptable strategies for managing risks and capitalizing on opportunities.

Promoting Innovation as a Core Value: Innovation should be at the heart of business strategy. Setting up an effective innovation management system encourages creative thinking and turns novel ideas into actionable projects. Additionally, building strategic partnerships with other companies, startups, and academic institutions can enhance an organization's innovative capabilities by providing access to new ideas, technologies, and markets.

Evaluating and Enhancing Business Strategies

To ensure continued relevance and competitiveness, businesses must engage in regular strategy reviews. These reviews are crucial for adjusting strategies to align with current realities and anticipated future conditions. Utilizing business analytics and robust feedback mechanisms, managers are able to assess the effectiveness of existing strategies comprehensively. This ongoing evaluation allows for informed adjustments, ensuring that the organization remains agile and responsive to market dynamics and consumer needs. Moreover, integrating sustainability into business practices is not just about fulfilling environmental and social responsibilities; it also enhances economic stability. By adopting sustainable practices, companies can improve their reputation and appeal to a growing base of consumers who prioritize environmental and social considerations in their purchasing decisions. This strategic alignment with sustainability not only contributes to the long-term viability of the business but also supports the broader goal of sustainable development.

Future-proofing your business demands a proactive and dynamic approach, emphasizing continuous learning, adaptation, and innovation. This chapter has detailed essential strategies that managers can implement to ready their organizations for forthcoming challenges and opportunities. By embracing these practices, businesses are well-positioned to succeed in the ever-evolving global market. They can lead their teams with foresight and agility, ensuring long-term success and sustainability. The guidance offered in this chapter serves as a comprehensive roadmap for leaders striving to construct resilient businesses that can adeptly navigate future challenges. By employing strategic confidence and innovative prowess, these leaders can ensure their organizations not only withstand but also thrive amidst the complexities of the modern business environment. This forward-thinking approach is critical for maintaining relevance and achieving sustained growth in an increasingly competitive landscape.

APPENDIX

This appendix serves as a supplementary resource for readers of "Navigating the Business Maze: Essential Management Skills for Today's Leaders." It includes additional tools, templates, case studies, and glossaries that complement the content found within the book. The goal of this appendix is to provide practical resources that can be directly applied to enhance understanding and implementation of the management skills discussed.

A. Management Tools and Templates

Strategic Planning Template: A step-by-step guide to help managers formulate and execute strategic plans.

Leadership Style Assessment: A questionnaire to help managers identify their leadership style and understand its impact on team dynamics.

Conflict Resolution Framework: A tool to aid in the structured resolution of workplace conflicts.

Negotiation Checklist: A checklist that outlines key steps and considerations before entering negotiation sessions.

Innovation Project Proposal Template: A template to help managers structure proposals for new projects or initiatives.

B. Detailed Case Studies

Tech Startup Scaling: Explores the challenges and strategies of a tech startup rapidly scaling its operations and team.

Turnaround of a Manufacturing Plant: Examines the leadership and management decisions involved in turning around an underperforming manufacturing facility.

Implementation of a CSR Initiative: Details the steps a company took to develop and implement a successful corporate social responsibility program.

C. Glossary of Terms

Agile Management: A methodical approach to software development that promotes continuous iteration of development and testing throughout the lifecycle of the project.

Empathetic Leadership: A leadership style that involves understanding, caring about, and considering the emotional states of others.

ROI (Return on Investment): A performance measure used to evaluate the efficiency or profitability of an investment.

Blockchain Technology: A system of recording information in a way that makes it difficult or impossible to change, hack, or cheat the system.

Stakeholder Engagement: The process by which an organization involves people who may be affected by the decisions it makes or can influence the implementation of its decisions.

D. Recommended Reading and Resources

To further enhance your understanding and skills in management, leadership, and related topics, here are some recommended readings and resources:

Books:

"Good to Great: Why Some Companies Make the Leap...And Others Don't" by Jim Collins - Explores what differentiates top companies from the rest.

"Leaders Eat Last: Why Some Teams Pull Together and Others Don't" by Simon Sinek - Discusses the role of leadership in building successful teams.

"The Lean Startup: How Today's Entrepreneurs Use Continuous Innovation to Create Radically Successful Businesses" by Eric Ries - Offers strategies for efficient business model testing and development.

"Dare to Lead: Brave Work. Tough Conversations. Whole Hearts." by Brené Brown - Focuses on developing courage and building effective leadership.

Journals:

Harvard Business Review - Offers articles on management, leadership, and business strategy.

The Journal of Change Management - Provides insights on theories and practices in change management.

Journal of Business Ethics - Discusses various aspects of ethics in business and corporate governance.

Online Resources:

MIT Sloan Management Review (https://sloanreview.mit.edu/) - Provides modern strategies and research on management practices.

McKinsey Insights (https://www.mckinsey.com/featured-insights) - Offers research and articles on various business management topics.

E. FAQs

Q1: What are some effective conflict resolution strategies in the workplace?

A1: Key strategies include active listening, seeking to understand all perspectives, addressing issues directly and respectfully, and finding common ground to formulate mutually beneficial solutions.

Q2: How can I develop my leadership skills?

A2: Continuous learning through courses and seminars, seeking feedback from peers and mentors, practicing self-reflection, and leading by example are effective ways to enhance your leadership abilities.

Q3: What are some tips for effective communication in a diverse team?

A3: Emphasize clarity and simplicity in communication, be mindful of cultural differences, use multiple communication platforms to ensure inclusivity, and encourage feedback to improve communication strategies.

F. Online Resources

Professional Organizations:

Project Management Institute (PMI)
(https://www.pmi.org/) - Offers resources and certifications for project managers.

American Management Association (AMA) (https://www.amanet.org/) - Provides a plethora of training and resources for management professionals.

Society for Human Resource Management (SHRM) (https://www.shrm.org/) - Useful for HR professionals and managers interested in developing their team management skills.

Educational Platforms:

Coursera (https://www.coursera.org/) - Offers online courses from leading universities on topics ranging from leadership to financial management.

LinkedIn Learning (https://www.linkedin.com/learning/) - Features courses in business, technology, and creative content aimed at professionals.

TED Talks (https://www.ted.com/topics/leadership) - Provides inspirational talks on leadership and management from experts and leaders worldwide.